CUT THE Sh*t

CUT THE Sh*t

33 Ways To Stop Having Insignificant Thoughts and Polish Your Mindset

STERLING CLINTON-SPELLMAN, The PolisHER

CUT THE SH*T
Published by Purposely Created Publishing Group™
Copyright © 2017 Sterling Clinton-Spellman

All rights reserved.

No part of this book may be reproduced, distributed or transmitted in any form by any means, graphics, electronics, or mechanical, including photocopy, recording, taping, or by any information storage or retrieval system, without permission in writing from the publisher, except in the case of reprints in the context of reviews, quotes, or references.

Printed in the United States of America
ISBN: 978-1-947054-04-2

Special discounts are available on bulk quantity purchases by book clubs, associations and special interest groups. For details email:
sales@publishyourgift.com
or call (888) 949-6228.

For information logon to:
www.PublishYourGift.com

DEDICATION

I dedicate this book to *you*! Nothing happens by chance—something about this book resonated with you and that's the reason it is in your possession now. I want you to know that I see you and feel you. No matter where you are in your journey, remember that you have the power to create the life of your dreams. It all starts with changing your mind! Remember these words:

> "Your beliefs become your thoughts,
> Your thoughts become your words,
> Your words become your actions,
> Your actions become your habits,
> Your habits become your values,
> Your values become your destiny."
>
> —Mahatma Gandhi

TABLE OF CONTENTS

Foreword – Aprille Franks-Hunt 1

Introduction 5

1. Make a Decision 13
2. Replace Your Old Thoughts With New Ones 15
3. Free Yourself from Other People's Opinions 17
4. Stop Asking for Permission 19
5. Give Yourself Permission 21
6. Be the Lead in Your Life 23
7. Focus on the Significant Things—
   What Really Matters 25
8. Think Kind Things About Yourself 27
9. Speak Kind Things About Yourself 29

10. Tap into the God in You 31

11. Believe in Your Worth 33

12. Think Big 35

13. Think Simple 37

14. Take Action 38

15. Invest in Your Personal Development 40

16. Invest in a Coach and Training 42

17. Invest in Your Self-Care 44

18. Feed Your Mind, Body, and Spirit 46

19. Get Inspired: Fill Your Cup and
    Pour Into Yourself 49

20. Invest in Experiences 51

21. Inspire Yourself 53

22. Level-Up Your Relationships 55

23. Be Grateful and Practice Gratitude Daily 57

24. Girl, Forgive Yourself 59

25. Evict the Bitch in Your Head 61

26. Refuse to Settle for Mediocre
    Thinking and Living 63

27. Seek Outside Help 65

28. Quit What No Longer Inspires You 67

29. Reclaim Your Dreams 69

30. Write Your Vision 71

31. Exercise Your Confidence Muscle 73

32. Keep a Wins/Success Journal 75

33. Focus On Your Purpose 77

Outro 79

About the Author 81

FOREWORD

Aprille Franks-Hunt

I think back to February 2008 in Columbus, MS. I was sitting across from a man from Long Beach, California, who had given me an opportunity to make $21,000 in thirty days that would ultimately change my life. He didn't know that's what the opportunity was, but I did.

I was going to be paid for doing the same job in sales that I was previously fired from just seven months prior. At that time, I literally had sixty dollars to my name, was living in the corporate housing they provided me, was driving a car I hadn't paid a car note on in over six months, and was unable to financially care for my eleven-year-young daughter. While my reality was broke, uncertain, and inflammatory, my mindset was far from it. I knew that I had to be mind-strong despite of the reality I woke up to on a daily basis.

This knowledge came from an inner knowing that my best was yet to come, from my unwavering faith, and from a movie I'd seen just the year before, *The Secret*. *The Secret* cemented what church didn't for me: It gave me "the how" to have more faith and to be deeply rooted in the actions of applying faith in everything I did.

When I think about success and the desire to want more, I often think on how our society encourages the "You can't do this because..." or "Who are you to think you can be successful?" rhetoric. I understand how the images in the media (both traditional and social), your past trials, and your current circumstances can play tricks on you. I understand that those things can make you believe the worst about yourself and your ability to have abundance, peace, and success in your life. I think about all of the men and women who buy into these falsehoods and allow them to become the real reasons as to why they can't improve or change. At the end of the day, we all have to cut out the sh*t that is not serving us: Bad habits, old patterns, beliefs systems, friends, sometimes family, and mindsets that are not conducive to achieving to the life we actually want. We all must own up to the fact that we have more control over our now and our future than we sometimes want to admit.

You see it daily: Motivational quotes from thought leaders encouraging you to develop your mindset and get on a new track. But that's not enough. Truth is, no matter what you say, your thoughts do create your reality and they are so powerful that, each day, it is laying the bricks for the foundation of your destiny. Though you may have heard these expressions over and over again, my question to you is, do you subscribe to that way of being? If not, by the time you finish this book, you will. This is one of the most important things you should subscribe to because it teaches you that you and you alone have the power to create the life you desire!

In this book, Sterling has captured the key steps you must take to master your thoughts, to pay attention to the significance of your life, and to provoke positive change. Cutting the sh*t is exactly what you must do if you want a mindset that fosters growth into a greater version of who you are—the you who is waiting for you to catch up to it. I urge you to not only allow her words to seep into your heart and mind, but also take advantage of the reflections and practice the affirmations to begin polishing your mindset. The sooner you master your thoughts, you will be able to start intentionally designing the life you always wanted to live.

I know firsthand that cutting out certain things and incorporating positive habits can drastically change your life for the better. You don't have to take my word for it—do it for yourself and implement the teachings in this book, then watch your own life transformation right before your eyes. Sterling is paving the way in a practical, simple, and effective way!

Now, time to cut the shi*!

INTRODUCTION

Hey, hey, hey, diamond!

I call you a diamond because I believe we all have the potential to shine as bright as the brightest diamond. Shining bright means allowing yourself to go through the process of transforming into the best version of yourself. Take note of how a diamond is created: It is formed from high pressure, chipping away at the unneeded debris and smoothing the rough edges. We see it shine so brightly and have incredible value because of what it has been through it. The same goes for you! Your true essence, beauty, and greatness have always been there but, sometimes, we have to withstand pressure and chip away at those things that are not necessary in our lives to truly shine at our brightest.

So, my beautiful diamond, I am happy you are here and have decided to *Cut the SH*T*!I am so excited to share my inner thoughts and experiences with you. Changing my mindset is one of the best things I have done for myself and I know doing so can transform your life too!

As a retired school teacher, I am an educator at heart. I love to teach, share information, and watch my students and now clients get "a-ha!" moments: Their faces light up, spirits rise, and overall joy encapsulates their minds because they finally get it! Moments like those have always been the reason why I teach. And since my transition to full-time entrepreneurship about nine months ago, I have had the great honor of teaching and sharing my gifts and talents with thousands of people via my coaching programs, online academy, books, speaking engagements, live events, workshops, and social media networks. I am so happy to share this message of polishing the mindset with you.

To succeed in any area of our life, the first thing we have to do is change our mindset. . Like the great Les Brown says,

> "There is nothing as powerful as a changed mind. You can change your hair, your clothing, your zip code, your spouse but if you do not change your mindset you will perpetuate the same experience over and over again because everything outwardly changed but nothing inwardly changed."

This has been proven true in my life, time and time again! You see, I am a pretty positive person, and most people would consider me to be an optimist. I am the woman who says, "When life gives you lemons, make lemonade. Better yet, I betcha we can think up a tool that can make lemonade flow like a river." Yes, that is me! I truly believe that anything is possible. .

But that is not to say that negative thinking and thoughts never ravish my mind and try to get the best of me. Yes, this is my confession! I, too, am sometimes tormented with thoughts that stop me dead in my tracks and prevent me from taking the necessary action for me to lead and shine bright in my life. Downright insignificant thoughts that, when I finally snap out of them, immediately become laughable. Because all those negative thoughts are false! In my spiral, my mind makes things up about stuff that hasn't happened, probably would never happen, and, if they did happen, would not be that big of a deal! But when in that negative trance, boy is it hard to see those things as non-factors.

What do insignificant thoughts look like?

- I am too old
- I am too young
- I am too fat

- I don't have a degree
- I am so over qualified
- I don't understand technology
- What if I mess up?
- What if I fail?
- Who is going to listen to me?
- Who am I to write a book?

Now, let's stop and think: In the grand scheme of things, do any of these things really matter? Will they really stop you from accomplishing your goal or do they just represent excuses that you have created for yourself?

I will never forget the day I attended a conference called Get Radical, hosted by Doreen Rainey. Lisa Nichols of the movie, *The Secret*, was speaking. I stood up to ask Lisa a question about how to start my business and get focused. I remember I said, "I keep starting and stopping," and she replied, "You know exactly what it is you want to do but your excuses got Swarovski crystals on them!" She pulled my card in front of all these folks—and she was right! Sometimes, we make our excuses sound so real and so sexy that we don't even recognize them as excuses. The other truth bomb she dropped was this: "You are so brilliant that your 10% of effort is better than some people's 100%. So, you continue to play small out of fear of shining too bright!"

Hello! Where did she know me from? She straight up described me to the T and, more importantly, she pointed out that I needed to get my mind right. I needed to work on my belief system and to focus on having a mindset that reflected my true essence. I know that many of you have the same struggles with mindset, self-worth, and following through on your dreams. Yes, some things may be temporary obstacles to your goals, but they should not stop your overall progression. I know curbing negative thoughts is easier said than done but it is possible.

So, let's talk about polishing your mindset! Because our mindsets are direct correlations with how successful we will be, it is extremely important to have a plan and way of thinking that serves and develops the best version, the magic, the God, the highest, most beautiful, and most divine version of You: A mindset focused on significant thoughts.

A polished mindset reflects the refinement of your attitude towards things you want and need to improve in your life. I have collected thirty-three tried and true ways to polish your mindset so you can stop having insignificant thoughts. I chose thirty-three because it represents how many years I have been on this earth and all the lessons I have learned about changing my own mindset to reflect success, abundance, health, wealth, prosperity, happiness, and love. These are implementable steps for everyday improvement. Remember, all change starts in the mind!

Cut the SH*T: 33 Ways To Stop Having Insignificant Thoughts and Polish Your Mindset is all about overcoming the negative and small thinking that paralyzes our success before we even start. This book will act as a guide filled with important reflective questions to ask yourself and affirmations to help you polish your mindset. I have defined for you some of the most important words we will use in this book. Though you probably know, hear, and use these words all the time, I created a word bank for reference throughout your reading.

Cut the SH*T Word Bank

WORD	DICTIONARY DEFINITION	HOW WORD IS USED IN THIS BOOK
SHIT	noun: 1. Feces. 2. A contemptible or worthless person verb: 1. Expel feces from the body 2. Tease or try to deceive (someone) exclamation: 1. An exclamation of disgust, anger, or annoyance	SHIT is an acronym for: **S**top **H**aving **I**nsignificant **T**houghts
Insignificant	adjective: 1. Too small or unimportant to be worth consideration 2. Without power or influence	Unimportant, trivial, trifling
Significant	adjective: 1. Sufficiently great or important to be worthy of attention; noteworthy 2. Having a particular meaning; indicative of something	Remarkable, important, worthy

Mindset	noun: 1. The established set of attitudes held by someone 2. An attitude, disposition, or mood 3. An intention or inclination	A collection of the dominant thoughts in your life
Polish	verb: 1. To improve; refine 2. Smoothing and brightening through friction	To remove the negative perception from life experiences that make you feel tarnished by creating shifts in your mindset to uncover your true essence.
POLISHED	adjective 1. Made smooth and glossy 2. Naturally smooth and glossy 3. Refined, cultured, or elegant	An acronym and the name of my company: **P**urpose **O**pportunity **L**ead **I**nspire/Impact **S**hine Bright **H**elp yourself/others **E**xperience life **D**ream Awake
POLISHED Mindset	There was no phrase to express what I was thinking so I created it!	A mindset that reflects the refinement of your attitude towards things you want and need to improve in your life.

1. Make a Decision

At some point, you are going to have to decide that enough is enough. That you are tired of putting your dreams on hold month after month, year after year. Each day we allow our entire being to be ravished by insignificant thoughts is another twenty-four-hours wasted. Remember, insignificant thinking is a sign that you are thinking small. You were not born to think small! There is a great vision for your life and thinking small will only prevent you from ever living up to that potential. You have to make the decision to cut the SHIT.

Reflect:

- What insignificant thoughts have I been replaying in my mind?
- How many hours, days, weeks, months, and years of my life am I giving to insignificant thoughts?

- Am I ready to make a decision to Stop Having Insignificant Thoughts?

Affirm:

Today I make a decision to Stop Having Insignificant Thoughts! There is a greater vision for my life!

2.
Replace Your Old Thoughts With New Ones

Remember the old saying that says, "The fastest way to get over a man is to replace him with a new one?" All that time, energy, and attention can be given to your new boo! But they forget to tell you that, if you do not deal with the baggage or old behavior that went on in the previous relationship, you may still suffer the same issues you had with boo number one.

The same goes when replacing your old insignificant thoughts with new significant thoughts. It's a great start but your shift will be short-lived if you do not put in the, work, work, work! Dragging in old habits and ways of thinking will only taint your new thoughts and thwart your efforts.

The next 31 ways to Stop Having Insignificant Thoughts will be all about doing the *work* to polish our minds and have thoughts that lead to success.

Reflect:

- What insignificant thoughts can I replace with significant thoughts?

Affirm:

I am ready and willing to do the work to replace insignificant thoughts with significant thoughts that lead to the greatest version of me.

3.
Free Yourself from Other People's Opinions

It is fascinating how much we allow what others think or feel dictate how we make decisions about our relationships, personal choices, or professional and career goals. We allow a person who has never run a business to determine what makes a good business plan or idea. We could just let them talk and talk, but the problem is, we allow people's negativity to control how we feel about ourselves and what we are capable of.

As you begin to focus on polishing your mind and living the life you desire, everyone and their momma will have something to say about what you should be doing. So, you *must* take a stand and value your own opinion. Have a rock-solid belief in yourself, your magic, your gifts, and your talents! Block out the naysayers and haters, because, if you think about it, what other people think about you is really none of your business.

Reflect:

- Am I allowing other people's opinions to dictate my life?

- Do I believe in my magic?

Affirm:

My opinion of myself and the way I live my life is what matters most! What other people think about me is none of my business!

4.
Stop Asking for Permission

There are many things you may want to do or try, but you may hesitate before even starting because you feel like you have to ask someone for permission. For instance, you want to be a public speaker but you are waiting for someone to designate you as a speaker at their event before you start doing that work.

I'll let you in on a secret: You *do not* need anyone else's permission to do anything, especially if that decision will propel you to live your dreams. After all, you and you alone are the only one who can deliver your God-given gifts and talents to the world.

If you want to be a public speaker, position yourself as one. Practice speaking, seek engagements, and create your own speaking platforms and events. This is exactly what I did to grow my speaking business. Do not wait for someone to give you permission because here is what happens: When you ask people for permission to live your dreams and your life, in most cases, you will live accordingly and bound to them. Who are they to tell you what to do?

Remember from the last chapter that other people's thoughts (especially negative ones) are insignificant to your thoughts. As you work on polishing your mindset, make sure someone else's thoughts do not cloud or overpower your own.

Reflect:

- What am I seeking permission for and who am I seeking permission from?
- Does asking for permission benefit or harm me in my situation?

Affirm:

I do not need someone else's permission to deliver my God-given gifts and talents to the world. I am enough!

5.

Give Yourself Permission

Now that you know that other people's permission and "allowance" is insignificant to your growth and success, let's talk about giving yourself permission to shine! I believe one of the best things you can do is to validate yourself. In recognizing and honoring your talents and affirmations, you will begin to believe and understand that you are worthy of all your heart's desires. Anything you want to achieve is obtainable—you just have to give yourself permission to be you! Give yourself permission to think big and to follow your dreams. Nothing can stop you when you call the shots.

Reflect:

- What are three things I can give myself permission to do or think today?

Affirm:

I give myself permission to create and live the life of my dreams! I have the keys to my success through my thoughts. What I think is what I will create and manifest!

6. Be the Lead in Your Life

One of my mentors Doreen Rainey said, "People don't usually force us out of the driver seat of our life. We move over and allow them to drive."

When I heard this, I thought to myself, "Lord, deliver me now!" I lived this way for so long. I allowed other people's happiness and joy to take the lead in my life. I would do things just to please other people, even if it was something I did not want to do. I was putting everyone else's needs and wants before my own, and people-pleasing had become a priority in my life.

You must learn to take the lead in your own life. If you want to be the best version of yourself and be happy, you must put yourself and your needs first. I am also talking to you mommies out there—I know that, as mothers, we often feel guilty when we attempt to put our needs before those of our children. But think about it this way: If you do not have what you need, will you be able to function at full capacity to be the best of mommy for your children? No!

Make sure you are putting yourself first by leading your life and doing the things that feel good to you. It will allow you to be at your best, which is also beneficial for people who matter most to you.

Reflect:

- Am I allowing other people's needs and wants take the lead in my life?
- What can I do today to put myself first?

Affirm:

I lead my life! My needs and wants are important, and I am important enough to put myself first.

7.

Focus on the Significant Things – What Really Matters

This entire book is about shifting away from insignificant thoughts and polishing your mindset to focus on significant thoughts. So, what are significant thoughts? Significant thoughts are those that really matter in creating and manifesting the life you desire. Essentially, these are productive and usable thoughts that don't stop you or discourage you. What really matter are your dreams, visions, and aspirations, so your thoughts must act as support! Those are the things that should be at the forefront of your mind. If you focus on what really matters, you won't have room for the things that don't matter.

Reflect:

- What are some of my dreams, visions, and aspirations? Are my thoughts supporting these aspects of me?

- What two thoughts can I focus on to develop into the best version of myself?

- How can I change insignificant thoughts into significant ones?

Affirm:

I create and manifest my success with my thoughts!

8.
Think Kind Things About Yourself

Thinking kind things about myself is one of my favorite things to do now, but it took a lot of practice at first. In fact, I know that many people struggle to think kind thoughts about themselves; they are not conditioned to think positively about themselves because doing so is labeled as arrogant. As a result, you may ignore amazing things about yourself and focus on the not-so-flattering things that lead to unkind and straight jacked-up thinking about yourself.

I had to learn to fall in love with myself and that was impossible without thinking kindly and lovingly about myself. I started to list all the things I loved about myself, beginning with my smile, the gap in my teeth, my hips, my loving heart, and my warm and infectious spirit. I wrote them on sticky notes and put them around my house and work desk so I could focus on those amazing things about me. And it worked!

Reflect:

- What are some amazing things about myself?
- What would I put on sticky notes and where can I put them up?

Affirm:

I am so in love with myself!

9. Speak Kind Things About Yourself

Gandhi once said, "Your thoughts become your words."

What you think will always find a way to escape your mouth. This is especially the case with anger. I often hear people say things like, "I am so stupid," "I am so broke," "I am so fat," "I will never be successful," "I will never get married," or the one that I hate the most "FML (fuck my life)." You say all those things casually, but you rarely realize that they are detrimental to your success.

Your words are powerful so you must be careful about what you speak over your life. This is why you must practice thinking then *speaking* kind things about yourself. You must remember that life and death is in the power of the tongue. Affirm the things you want, and speak joy, positivity, success, and love over your life.

Reflect:

- What are some things that I say that are not life-giving?

- What kind of things should I be saying instead?

Affirm:

What I say is powerful, so I choose to speak positivity over my life!

10. Tap into the God in You

Do you know you are wonderfully made? That you are an uniquely designed, unrepeatable miracle? There is no one else who exists on this earth like you. Nobody can do you like *you* do you. No one has the exact gifts and talents that you do, because you are a magnificent being made in the image of our Creator. Not only should that encourage you, but it should also remind and inspire you that there is nothing you can't do thanks to the God in you.

Because the work of God must be done on earth and miracles must take place, we must tap into the God who created us. Once you believe in the God in you, your purpose will show up and you will understand that anything is possible. Then, you must fulfill that purpose for God's will to be done.

Reflect:

- Do I know I am wonderfully made?
- What are some unique qualities, gifts, and talents that I possess?
- How can I worship the God in myself?

Affirm:

I am wonderfully made, so I celebrate the God in me!

11. Believe In Your Worth

When I think about the idea of being worthy I think about these two quotes:

> *"Self-worth comes from one thing – thinking that you are worthy."*
>
> **—Wayne Dyer**

> *"You're imperfect, and you're wired for struggle, but you are worthy of love and belonging."*
>
> **—Brene Brown**

Because of the struggles or negative experiences you go through, you may have a tarnished view of your worth. You may feel like you do not deserve success, love, happiness, money, or peace, because you have not been afforded those things adequately before. You have to remember that, just because you went through a rough patch in your life *does not* make you broken or worth less. A crumpled up and stained $100 bill is still worth $100. The true essence or value of a piece of silver does not lessen just because it is a little tarnished. All it needs is a little bit of polishing to uncover the true beauty.

Polish your true self, honor the God within, and believe in your worth! You deserve to live a purposeful life and to see your dreams manifest.

Reflect:

- Why might I have a tarnished view of my worth?
- Why am I worthy of living the life I desire?

Affirm:

I am worthy of success! I am worthy of love! I am worthy of happiness!

12.
Think Big

My idea of thinking big is thinking outside of the box. As a matter of fact, I want you to forget the box. Create your own way.

Thinking big and in my own way has been one of the best things I have ever done. Once your mind is expanded and you begin to think up big, freaking amazing ideas, it is difficult for you to revert back to small, lacking thoughts Once you allow yourself to free your mind and explore your dreams, you will come up with bold ideas that other people may not understand. But remember, that vision was given to you, so if they do not understand your ideas or plans, that's totally fine! It is not for them to understand—the only opinion that truly matters is yours.

Reflect:

- What are some big ideas I have been thinking about?

Affirm:

I am in love with thinking outside the box and creating my own way!

13.
Think Simple

Just because you are thinking big doesn't mean your ideas have to be complicated. We sometimes overthink or overcomplicate things because we think the simple way is too easy, thus is not a valuable idea. Not true at all. Complicating things will only frustrate you. Simplify your big ideas by creating the easiest and most repeatable way to execute your intentions. Enough said!

Reflect:

- How can I simplify my big ideas?

Affirm:

Simple is powerful!

14. Take Action

What is it that you want to do for your life? Are just dreaming and thinking? If so, you must take actual action now! Making small, daily moves gets you closer to your dream but also reinforces your positive self-image, because you will start viewing yourself as someone who makes things happen. You are no longer waiting on the perfect opportunity to start; instead, you are creating opportunities to manifest your dreams. Take note from this quote by Dale Carnegie, "Inaction breeds doubt and fear. Action breeds confidence and courage. If you want to conquer fear, do not sit home and think about it. Go out and get busy."

Reflect:

- What are things that I've been dreaming about but haven't yet tried?

- What are two things I can take action on today to get myself one step closer to accomplishing my goals?

Affirm:

I am an action-taker! I create opportunities that help me manifest my dreams!

15.

Invest in Your Personal Development

Personal development is all about reframing your mindset through developing your knowledge, interests, thoughts, and self. The more you grow as a person, the more you stretch and mold your mindset. Investing in your personal development is also a great way to increase your self-confidence.

The important thing to remember about personal development is that you must practice it daily. Learning and growing must become a habit. Why? Because wherever you go, there you are, waiting to be cultivated.

One of the ways I invest in myself is through reading. Reading provides new ideas and a different perspective, and expands your horizon. I read devotionals, personal development books, business books, blogs, and magazines that support my growth. Also, try listening to different podcasts and watching YouTube videos that will prepare you for your next steps.

Reflect:

- What materials do I interact with everyday? Am I reading gossip magazines and negative news articles all day, everyday?

- What two new resources can I add to my list to enhance my personal development?

Affirm:

Personal development is a daily practice for me!

16.
Invest in a Coach and Training

I invest in coaching and training as parts of my personal and professional development. Every successful person I know and study with has a coach and puts his or her time, energy, and resources in guidance that supports growth.

A coach helps you understand and utilize your gifts and talents at your full potential. Training programs and coaching are what gave me the tools and resources to really take my business to the next level.

Let me be clear: Investing in coaching is not just a financial investment but also investments of your time and energy. Many people have coaches or buy programs and never do any of the work, which is waste of everyone's time. That means you must be willing to invest in yourself to actually take advantage of the coaching.

Reflect:

- In what area would I most benefit from coaching and training?
- Am I prepared to invest in myself?

Affirm:

Investing in coaching and training is in my best interest.

17.

Invest in Your Self-Care

Self-care is crucial to polishing your mind. So many people walk around completely burnt out, wondering why they resent everything and everyone in their lives. Self-care, or any act of loving oneself, promotes positive vibes toward yourself. Self-care can look like manicures and pedicures and massages, or simply a pocket of personal time to reflect on your goals and dreams, meditate, and speak your affirmations. The most important part of self-care is to take a break from the craziness of our day-to-day lives.

As a wife, mom, daughter, sister, friend, and business owner, I sometimes feel like making time for self-care seems impossible. But if I am burnt out, I am no good to anyone, including myself. If you do not invest in self-care, it will be difficult for you to see greater for yourself. So, find time every single day, even if it is ten to fifteen minutes, to just be still and focus on making love to yourself. Think, speak, and feel good things during that time. Once you master those ten to fifteen minutes a day of "me" time, start carving out bigger chunks of time to just focus on you!

Reflect:

- Am I showing myself love in the form of self-care?
- What sort of self-care do I want to practice?
- How can I create space for me to practice self-care daily?

Affirm:

I am worthy of spending time with myself. I deserve to think, speak and feel good things about myself!

18. Feed Your Mind, Body, and Spirit

Have you ever heard of the expression "Junk in, junk out?" That means that whatever you put into something is what you are going to get out. This statement is very true when it comes to our minds, bodies, and spirits, which all consume "food" in different ways. Thus, I believe in a holistic approach: You eat a healthy diet to keep your body healthy, think positive thoughts to keep your mind clear, and love yourself to keep your spirit open to receive. Every part of you is connected so you must pay attention to what you are feeding yourself, whether it be food, thoughts, or vibes. If you start slacking in one area, it will definitely affect another.

Here are some great ways to feed mind, body, and spirit daily:

Pray

- Get connected to your source. Prayer is your power connection to communicate with God and to discern His purpose for your life
- Be intentional
- Ask God for guidance in living in purpose
- Ask for the things you want and need
- Pray about all things and worry less

Meditate

- Pray is asking. Meditating is listening
- Listen for guidance
- Think clearly and refrain from getting stuck in one thought for too long
- Be still
- A series of Harvard University studies led by professor Sara Lazar proved that meditation practices actually create changes in the way the brain is wired and affects regions associated with stress, well-being, and intelligence.

Reflect:

- What am I feeding my mind, body, and spirit daily?
- What changes can I make about what I am putting *in* to get better results to come *out*?

Affirm:

I treat my mind, body, and spirit as one temple. I only consume good things.

19.

Get Inspired: Fill Your Cup and Pour into Yourself

I attend conferences and networking opportunities to get inspired, rejuvenate, and recommit myself to my goals. I try to attend at least one personal development or professional development conference once every quarter. My goal is always to learn something new and meet like-minded individuals who are on the same journey as me. Hearing their success stories reminds me of my own possibilities, which gives me the boost I need to continue investing in myself and pouring into my clients and relationships.

I also pour into myself through listening to podcasts or motivational videos daily. One of my all time favorite podcast is Rosetta Thurman's "Happy Black Woman." I love her podcast because she features Black women who are living their dreams. These women represent possibility to me and encourages me to look beyond the obstacles I may face.

I pour into myself daily because I intend to pour into others daily. Remember, it's not just about you! Like my mentor Lisa Nichols says, "You cannot serve from a bone-dry cup. Serve from your overflow!" You goal should be to always be in overflow.

Reflect:

- How can I fill my cup daily?
- Do I allow myself to be poured into?
- What is my overflow and how can it serve others?

Affirm:

I allow myself to be poured into daily because I intend to pour into others daily! I serve from my overflow!

20. Invest in Experiences

Experiences are so important for your overall growth and is most beneficial to expanding and stretching your mind. I rather spend my time and resources on experiences that I can learn from than on material things that will not have a lasting impact. Mark Twain said it best: "Twenty years from now, you will be more disappointed by the things you didn't do than by the ones you did do, so throw off the bowlines, sail away from safe harbor, catch the trade winds in your sails.

Explore, dream, discover."

Your experiences will teach you more about yourself and life in general than any material item, since those events and lessons come together to create your perspective on life. Imagine if you never traveled, took up a dance class, went to a museum, or visited an innovative restaurant. Imagine how limited your view of the world would be.

Traveling to different countries and states, attending cultural affairs, and participating in all kinds of business conferences have shaped me into the well-rounded and progressive businesswoman I am today. Take time to experience life!

Reflect:

- What new experience will I take advantage of this month?
- What can I learn from that experience?

Affirm:

I love new experiences and I embrace the new perspectives that I gain from them!

21.

Inspire Yourself

Inspiring yourself is important yet easy to neglect. Sometimes, you work so hard to be inspiring to others that you forget to inspire yourself! Celebrate and recognize who you are. Do things that you actually love and make you happy, and test your boundaries.

Pay attention to your successes because they will serve as a reminder of how far you have come and will inspire you to keep pushing through the not-so-sexy times during your journey. I inspire myself by reading through my old journals or listening to interviews I have done; then. I say to myself, "Girl, you are simply amazing. Nobody can do it like you!"

Reflect:

- What inspires me about myself?
- How can I use those inspirations?

Affirm:

I am inspired by me!

22.
Level-Up Your Relationships

Form and nurture relationships with people who are aligned with your goals. Find people who are on the same path as you or are already where you would like to go. Having friends, supportive Facebook groups, and masterminds throughout my transition process has been a blessing and an integral part of my success.

Intentionally put yourself around people who you strive to learn from and you can have mutually supportive relationships with. Be around people who stretch you! You always hear the expression, "If you are the smartest person in your group, you need a new group of friends." It is the truest statement ever. If all your friends do is complain about what they don't have or about the latest and greatest reality TV show, you may want to limit your time with them. Spend your precious hours with the people who support and encourage your growth and less with those who undermine your worth.

Reflect:

- How can I upgrade my relationships?
- Where can I find a tribe of people who can stretch me and vice versa?

Affirm:

I have valuable relationships that are mutually beneficial!

23.

Be Grateful and Practice Gratitude Daily

Have an attitude of gratitude. In all things give thanks and be grateful, because, if you look, there is so much around you to be thankful for. If you woke up this morning, if you have clean water to drink, if you have a place to lay your head at night, if at least one person loves you, if you have access to a computer and/or a cellphone, if you have legs to walk on, hands to clap with, and a mouth to talk with, you are doing pretty amazing. If you make more than $34,000 a year, you are in the top 1% of the world. You may be living paycheck to paycheck, but you are still far better off than most. Never forget that many are not afforded the same simple pleasures and basic needs or rights.

So, why does this matter? It matters because we get so caught up in what we want and don't have that we forget to be grateful for what we do have. What you focus on is what you get more of. Try keeping a gratitude journal: With this practice, you must write down ten things you are grateful for each day for twenty-eight days straight. It is the most amazing feeling to be in gratitude all day. It is like nothing can ruin your day because you are too focused on all that is well. It is hard to be anything but happy when you are grateful.

Reflect:

- Am I grateful for all that I have?
- How can I practice gratitude daily?

Affirm:

I practice gratitude daily!

24.

Girl, Forgive Yourself

Lack of forgiveness will affect how you show up in the world. For me, I could not forgive myself for the abortion I had at eighteen and I mentally tortured myself for twelve years, walking in the shadow of my mistakes. I allowed an error I made when I was young, a mistake God had already forgiven me for, to stop me from living out my purpose and God's calling on my life. I eventually began hiding behind my mistakes, flying just below the radar and tip-toeing to success. I felt like, if I showed up big in the world, I would be vulnerable and the world would find out my secret.

Forgiveness is freedom. It does not happen overnight and you often don't forget. But, you must forgive. Today, do something radical! Start your process of forgiveness.

Girl, forgive yourself because your success depends on it. I want you to go find a mirror, look yourself in the eyes, and reflect on the thing or things you are holding on too. I want you to say to yourself, "I have made mistakes in my past, but today, I forgive you! I love you!" Repeat this twice a day when you look in the mirror until you truly believe it.

Reflect:

- What have I not forgiven myself for?
- Are my mistakes overshadowing my successes?

Affirm:

I have made mistakes in my past, but today, I forgive you! I love you!

25.
Evict the Bitch in Your Head

Sometimes, you can be own worst critic during your growth process. You are the person who has assaulted your character worse than any hater or naysayer in the world. The things you say to yourself, if another person said to you, a fistfight would ensue. I call that The Bitch or the mean girl in your head. The Bitch keeps reminding you of all your failures, forgotten promises, missed attempts, etc. Imagine walking around with someone next to you and, every time you tried to do something, she reminds you of that time you tried but it didn't work. Every time you are happy, she says, "Nope, girl, you got to worry about those bills. You better worry about this, that, and the other."

Well, guess what? Tell that negativity, "Bye Felicia! Sit down and be gone." You no longer have space for her to live in your head!

Reflect:

- What does The Bitch/mean girl in my head say to me?
- How can I excuse her from my life?

Affirm:

I no longer have space for The Bitch to live in my head.

26. Refuse to Settle for Mediocre Thinking and Living

When those insignificant thoughts try to creep up and infiltrate your mind, I want you to refuse to settle for them. They are not true representations of who you are. Instead, recognize that it is most likely fear showing up.

I am sure you have heard this before, that the word "fear" can represent False Evidence Appearing Real. Replace this insignificant thought: Make FEAR represent "Face Everything And Rise." It's up to you to upgrade your thinking and make the decision of what you want situations to be in your life. When things don't go your way, do you let that situation be a failure or a lesson? Will you push past the fear?

Don't settle for the mediocre thought. You always have a choice !

Reflect:

- What mediocre thoughts try to infiltrate my mind?
- How can I upgrade those thoughts and find the lessons in them?

Affirm:

I refuse to settle for mediocre thinking!

27. Seek Outside Help

Sometimes, those insignificant and negative thoughts you have may be a sign that you need to seek professional help. You may be depressed or dealing with the aftermath of trauma. Do not be ashamed to get help. I know that, in the African/African American/Caribbean communities, it is taboo to see a psychiatrist or any mental or psychological professional. However, that secrecy and silence results in people continuing to suffer from mental illness or bottling up any and all emotions because of the fear of being seen as crazy.

Never mind what people think. Seek the help you need to feel and be your best.

Reflect:

- Would I benefit from speaking to a therapist or seeking professional help?
- What resources are available to me?

Affirm:

I deserve support!

28.
Quit What No Longer Inspires You

To most people, quitting has a negative connotation that they never want to be associated with. That was me: I stayed in bad relationships and toxic work environments all because I did not want to be viewed as a quitter. When I finally decided to quit my job last year, I had to embrace quitting! I was setting myself free from a situation that was no longer conducive to my well-being, and there was nothing negative about that.

Change your perspective on quitting. As Osayi Emokpae Lasisi says:

"Quitting is not giving up, it's choosing to focus your attention on something more important. Quitting is not losing confidence, it's realizing that there are more valuable ways you can spend your time. Quitting is not making excuses, it's learning to be more productive, efficient and effective instead. Quitting is letting go of things (or people) that are sucking the life out of you so you can do more things that will bring you strength."

Reflect:

- What are two things I can quit that will allow me to focus on the important things in my life?

- How can quitting benefit me?

Affirm:

I embrace quitting things that no longer serve me!

29.

Reclaim Your Dreams

Many people dream at night, which is great. But how many people dream while they are awake? When you dream awake, you have the boldness to *believe* that you can achieve those dreams. You put in work, you ask for help (not permission!), research, and keep pushing. When you fully understand and implement your dreams, you can literally change the trajectory of your life.

One day, I was driving behind our food truck on the way to the Pawtucket Farmers Market. I was reflecting on the importance of continuing to dream while you are awake. The Salad Man and Juice Bar Food Truck is literally a manifestation of a dream my husband, Russell, had one night a little over a year ago. I remember him waking up in the middle of the night shouting, "Salad Man and Juice Bar!"

I told him to go back to sleep, but he sat up and wrote it down. The next couple of months after that night, Russ started dreaming awake. He started researching food truck operations. He started drawing out the plans and design for the truck. I started looking for opportunities to network with other business people.

Here we are today, four years later. We just partnered with a multimillion-dollar company to market their products. Because we had the audacity to dream awake and put some action and sweat equity behind that dream, so many doors opened up for us. Now, we are living our dream of providing our community with delicious and healthy food. Other people are literally living in our dream. It is an amazing feeling to receive multiple emails a day from people requesting your service and saying, "Where have you been all my life?"

Don't worry about the how yet; instead, focus on the what. When you invest and believe in your dreams, doors will open for you. Today, choose to dream awake!

Reflect:

- What dreams have I been sleeping on?
- Do I really believe in my dreams?

Affirm:

I choose to dream awake! I have the audacity to believe in my dreams!

30.
Write Your Vision

You know there is a greater plan for your life but, sometimes, your insignificant thinking talk you out of paying attention to your vision. The best thing to do is to write your vision out. What is it that you want out of life? What do you see for yourself, your family, your community, and your legacy?

When writing your goals and aspirations down, be as detailed as possible. It should be so detailed that you can see, smell, hear, taste, and feel what you envision—let it all unfold without focusing on the how, what, or why it will or will not work. Writing your vision down takes the ideas out of your head and puts it on paper and out into the universe. So, set a timer for ten minutes and free-write your vision from your heart. After you write, put your vision in a place where you can see it and revisit it daily. Increase your chances of actually manifesting that vision!

Reflect:

- What is my vision for the next thirty days of my life?
- What is my vision for the next ninety days for my life?
- What is my vision for the next year and for the next five years of my life?
- What is my vision for the legacy I want to leave for my family and the world?

Affirm:

My vision matters and deserves to be written down and seen!

31.

Exercise Your Confidence Muscle

Confidence is like a muscle—you must use it or you will lose it. Take risks and step out on faith, give yourself credit for your part in success. Recognizing your achievements is not egotistical; it's healthy. It is a way of letting yourself know that you're stretching yourself and growing your confidence, that you're moving forward rather than running away.

Walk in your lane—what do I mean? I mean do what you do best. We are most confident when we are operating in our genius, when we know what we are talking about. Move within your strengths and comfort, all the while developing the skills in areas where you feel you are weak. That way, you can build confidence in all areas! Remember that being confident is an ongoing process;

it isn't a goal that you achieve and then stop pursuing. Keep exercising your muscle and your confidence will continue to grow. You will be surprised at how much your mindset changes for the better when you believe in yourself and know your worth.

Reflect:

- What can I do today to grow my confidence?
- Which skills do I want to develop and what areas do I want to grow in?
- How can I strengthen my confidence in that area?

Affirm:

I am confident! I exercise my confidence muscle daily!

32.
Keep a Wins/Success Journal

Keep a Wins/Success Journal to remind yourself that you are the epitome of the dragon slayer. Success can be quickly forgotten, which can make your journey frustrating. You may feel like you are not making progress, but when you look back at where you came from and the steps you have taken towards your goals, it can be a true motivator. Even if you look back at your journal and see that you are currently slacking, it should still be a motivator because it serves as proof that you did it before and can do it again!

Use journaling as an opportunity to write your vision and make it plain. A journal serves as a record of our progress. Write down your thoughts, dreams, visions, ideas, and, of course, your successes! I love this quote by

William Self: "Always carry a notebook. And I mean always. The short-term memory only retains information for three minutes; unless it is committed to paper, you can lose an idea forever."

Reflect:

- What wins/successes have I had in the last thirty days?

Affirm:

I own my wins! I own my success! I learn from my failures and mistakes! I celebrate it all!

33.

Focus On Your Purpose

What is purpose? What is *your* purpose? You probably hear it all the time and may wonder what yours is. When I think about purpose, I think about why something exists and the intention with which it was created.

Since I was a little girl, I knew my purpose was to inspire people. I wanted to and still want to help them uncover their true essence. Because I am aware of my purpose, I keep it in the forefront of my mind. I have affirmations, pictures, and vision boards in places where I can see them daily to remind me of why I exist and what intentions God has for me. So when the insignificant thoughts show up and I begin to shrink and think small, I remind myself of my greater purpose and how, if I deny myself the opportunity to walk in my purpose, I would block other people's blessings. If I do not operate in my purpose, the people who I am supposed to help will not get the polishing they need. The same goes for you. If you do not stay focused on your purpose, what happens to the people you are meant to bless with your gifts and talents?

As you are doing the work of polishing your mindset, make sure you focus on your purpose. Focus on how fulfilling and rewarding it is to walk in your calling and meaning. If you focus on your purpose, you will less likely focus on insignificant thoughts that keep you away from achieving your goals.

Reflect:

- What is my purpose?
- How do I keep it in the forefront of my mind?
- What is one thing I can do daily to focus on my purpose?

Affirm:

I am purpose-driven! I walk, think, and live in my purpose daily!

OUTRO

Changing your daily activities by implementing these thirty-three steps will drastically improve and POLISH your mindset. They will make you intentional about how and what you think about throughout your day. Before we end, I want to share with you one of my favorite quotes by Marianne Williamson. I hope it inspires you to lead and shine bright to inspire others through your newly polished mindset.

> "Our deepest fear is not that we are inadequate. Our deepest fear is that we are powerful beyond measure. It is our light, not our darkness that most frightens us. We ask ourselves, 'Who am I to be brilliant, gorgeous, talented, fabulous?' Actually, who are you not to be? You are a child of God. Your playing small does not serve the world. There is nothing enlightened about shrinking so that other people won't feel insecure around you. We are all meant to shine, as children do. We were born to make manifest the glory of God that is within us. It's not just in some of us;

it's in everyone. And as we let our own light shine, we unconsciously give other people permission to do the same. As we are liberated from our own fear, our presence automatically liberates others."

—**Marianne Williamson**

ABOUT THE AUTHOR

Sterling Clinton-Spellman, affectionately known as the "Polisher" and "Success Alchemist," is a renowned author, speaker, empowerment coach, and transformational business consultant.

Her mission is to guide individuals towards realizing their inherent greatness and living their dreams. With a wealth of experience in education, entrepreneurship, and personal development, Sterling brings a unique blend of insight and inspiration to her work. Through her books, workshops, speaking engagements, and consulting she has transformed countless lives and businesses.

To learn more, visit her website at
wwww.PolishedbySterling.com

CREATING DISTINCTIVE BOOKS WITH INTENTIONAL RESULTS

We're a collaborative group of creative masterminds with a mission to produce high-quality books to position you for monumental success in the marketplace.

Our professional team of writers, editors, designers, and marketing strategists work closely together to ensure that every detail of your book is a clear representation of the message in your writing.

Want to know more?
Write to us at info@publishyourgift.com
or call (888) 949-6228

Discover great books, exclusive offers, and more at
www.PublishYourGift.com

Connect with us on social media

@publishyourgift

www.ingramcontent.com/pod-product-compliance
Lightning Source LLC
Chambersburg PA
CBHW071535080526
44588CB00011B/1674